INVESTIGATING THE UNEXPLAINED

ESP

By Paige V. Polinsky

BELLWETHER MEDIA • MINNEAPOLIS, MN

Blastoff! Discovery launches a new mission: reading to learn. Filled with facts and features, each book offers you an exciting new world to explore!

This edition first published in 2020 by Bellwether Media, Inc.

No part of this publication may be reproduced in whole or in part without written permission of the publisher. For information regarding permission, write to Bellwether Media, Inc., Attention: Permissions Department, 6012 Blue Circle Drive, Minnetonka, MN 55343.

Library of Congress Cataloging-in-Publication Data

Names: Polinsky, Paige V., author.
Title: ESP / by Paige V. Polinsky.
Description: Minneapolis, MN : Bellwether Media, Inc., 2020.
   | Series: Blastoff! Discovery: Investigating the Unexplained |
   Includes bibliographical references and index.
Identifiers: LCCN 2019000960 (print) | LCCN 2019005905
   (ebook) | ISBN 9781618915818 (ebook) |
   ISBN 9781644870402 (hardcover : alk. paper)
Subjects: LCSH: Extrasensory perception–Juvenile literature.
Classification: LCC BF1321 (ebook) | LCC BF1321 .P65 2020
   (print) | DDC 133.8–dc23
LC record available at https://lccn.loc.gov/2019000960

Editor: Kate Moening   Designer: Andrea Schneider

Printed in the United States of America, North Mankato, MN.

TABLE OF CONTENTS

HIT
OR MISS

Li sits at a small desk. She studies a photo of three cows standing in a sunny field. A mountain fills the sky behind them. Li stares at the photo. She focuses on it with all her might.

Three rooms away, Omar sits at his desk with a blank piece of paper. He focuses on removing all thoughts from his mind. Then he starts to draw. His pencil flashes across the page for a few minutes. When he is finished, he takes the drawing to Li.

Omar hands Li the drawing. It looks like three spotted circles on a big triangle. She holds the paper up to five different photos. She studies each photo carefully and compares them to the drawing.

Li's eyes widen. The spotted circles in Omar's drawing match the placement of the cows in the photo she had been staring at. "That's a **hit**," Li says. "It's like you read my mind." Was it a lucky guess? Or does Omar really have ESP?

THE SIXTH SENSE

Have you ever had a dream that seemed to come true? Or known a person's thoughts before they said a word? If so, some say you might have extrasensory perception, or ESP.

HANDS OFF!

Some psychics claim to have "psychokinesis," or the ability to move objects with the mind. But psychokinesis is not a type of ESP. All ESP involves knowing things, not changing them.

TYPES OF ESP

TELEPATHY: Reading the thoughts of another person
Example: You guess the symbol on a hidden card.

CLAIRVOYANCE: Knowing information that is not necessarily known by any other person
Example: You guess the order of the shuffled cards.

PRECOGNITION: Predicting future events
Example: You guess the future order of cards about to be shuffled.

PSYCHOMETRY: Knowing information about a person or place by touching an object
Example: You guess where a deck of cards was bought by touching it.

Humans explore the world using the five senses. They are sight, smell, hearing, taste, and touch. But ESP is the ability to know things without using those senses. People with this "sixth sense" are often called psychics. They are known to read minds, see the future, or even talk to ghosts!

GHOSTS AND GUESSES

In the late 1800s, a religion called **Spiritualism** gained popularity. Spiritualists paid **clairvoyants** to speak with the dead. This practice sparked an interest in scientific ESP studies. In 1882, the Society for Psychical Research (SPR) formed in London. Its members used science to **investigate** clairvoyance and other claims of ESP.

The SPR questioned psychics carefully. In many tests, **subjects** were asked to guess the numbers on hidden playing cards. In 1911, American **parapsychologist** John Edgar Coover ran similar tests using numbered wooden blocks. But no experiments showed **evidence** of ESP.

AN ANCIENT IDEA

Psychic powers are an ancient belief. Aristotle wrote about the idea back in 350 BCE. He believed that some dreams saw into the future. But the term "ESP" was not used until 1870!

Despite the lack of evidence, some scientists were believers. Hans Berger thought **telepathy** was caused by electrical signals in the brain. In 1924, Berger became the first to record these signals in humans using an **electroencephalograph** (EEG). The EEG became an important medical tool. But few people used it to study ESP.

SNOOZING PSYCHICS

In 1962, a New York lab studied ESP in dreams. Researchers focused on pictures while subjects slept. They then studied whether the images in the pictures matched the subjects' dreams. Success rates were high! But the results could not be repeated.

J.B. Rhine

Card-guessing remained the standard testing method. Joseph Banks Rhine ran card tests during the 1930s. His results supported telepathy, but **skeptics** found many flaws. Investigators developed new ways to test ESP. But these methods did not show proof either!

Zener cards

PROFILE: THE DUKE UNIVERSITY EXPERIMENTS

In 1930, J.B. Rhine began card-guessing experiments with partners at Duke University. Scientist Karl Zener created special cards for the tests. Each card showed a simple shape.

A tester would hold a card out of sight. The subject then guessed its symbol. By 1934, Rhine's team had run 90,000 tests. Many subjects scored higher than they could have by chance. Skeptics blamed cheating and flawed cards. But Rhine stood by his results. His work made the term "ESP" popular.

GUESSING GAME

Zener cards soon became popular outside of the laboratory. By 1937, newsstands sold them for 10 cents a deck!

DUKE UNIVERSITY

Durham,
North Carolina

ESP research found fresh support in the 1970s during the **Cold War**. The United States wanted to try to run spy missions using psychics. But the government's **remote viewing** studies had mixed success.

LOST AND FOUND

In 1981, U.S. General James Dozier was kidnapped in Italy. The U.S. government hired psychic Joe McMoneagle to help find him. McMoneagle named a city, drew a street map, and described a building. Dozier was found before McMoneagle's tips arrived, but they were a perfect match.

HOW REMOTE VIEWING TESTS WORK

1. The sender goes to a secret location. They focus on a photo the viewer cannot see.

2. The viewer stays in the lab. They draw any images that come to mind.

3. The judge receives the drawing, the photo, and four different photos. They match the viewer's drawing to the photo that is most similar.

4. If the judge selects the sender's photo, it counts as a hit.

The experiment supports ESP if the judge makes more hits than are possible by chance.

In the early 1990s, scientists Daryl Bem and Charles Honorton ran a series of **ganzfeld experiments**. Their results supported ESP. But others could not repeat it. Bem created new tests with even stronger results! Bem shared the results in 2010, shocking other scientists. The methods were standard, but the **data** seemed impossible.

THOUGHT EXPERIMENTS

Parapsychologists are still investigating ESP. Instead of Zener cards, most researchers now use tools used in any scientific experiment. They log important details in computers. Cameras record experiments for later review.

EEG head cap

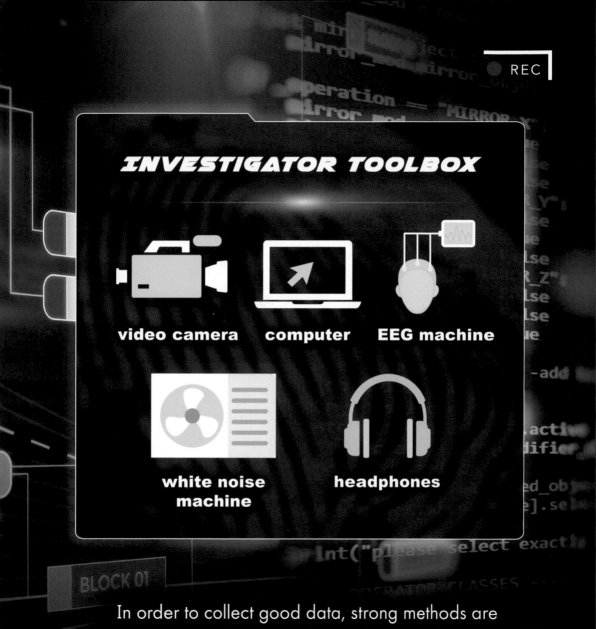

INVESTIGATOR TOOLBOX

video camera

computer

EEG machine

white noise machine

headphones

BLOCK 01

In order to collect good data, strong methods are more important than any other tool. Researchers

Faraday
cage

CAGE CONFUSION

Some scientists believe ESP signals come from
magnetic energy created by electricity. This is
called electromagnetic energy. Researchers may
place their subjects in an enclosure called a
Faraday cage. The cage blocks these waves. But
many studies show this has no effect.

ganzfeld experiment

Many parapsychologists believe the five senses drown out ESP. Ganzfeld experiments block the senses to make ESP stronger. Subjects sit in a room with their eyes covered. Headphones play **white noise**.

In a different room, "senders" focus on a photo. Meanwhile, subjects talk about any pictures that pop into their heads. Then subjects look at a set of photos and choose the one that best matches their thoughts. The sender's photo is considered a hit. Digital ganzfeld experiments use videos instead of photos.

device to measure sweat levels

Some researchers study the human body for signs of ESP. In one common study, the subject watches images flash on a computer screen. Some images are calm. Others are scary and upsetting.

large fear-response pupil

As the subject watches the screen, researchers measure their **pupil** size. Special devices also track how much subjects sweat. Fear makes pupils get bigger and makes people sweat more. But sometimes the change happens before the subject sees a scary image. Could this be ESP?

WHAT ARE THE ODDS?

Most scientists do not believe in ESP. They point out that humans have special **receptors** for each of the five senses. But no one has found a receptor for this sixth sense. How would our bodies process it?

Skeptics also point out that most reports of ESP are personal stories. Some claims can be tested. But not all experiments are good science. Subjects might cheat. Some researchers might change a study until they get the data they want. Others might leave failed tests out of their results.

WHO WANTS TO BE A MILLIONAIRE?

In 1964, magician James Randi made a challenge. If anyone showed him scientific evidence that they had ESP or similar powers, he would give them $1,000. Over time, the prize grew to $1 million. Randi challenged many famous psychics, but none accepted. He ended the offer in 2015.

James Randi

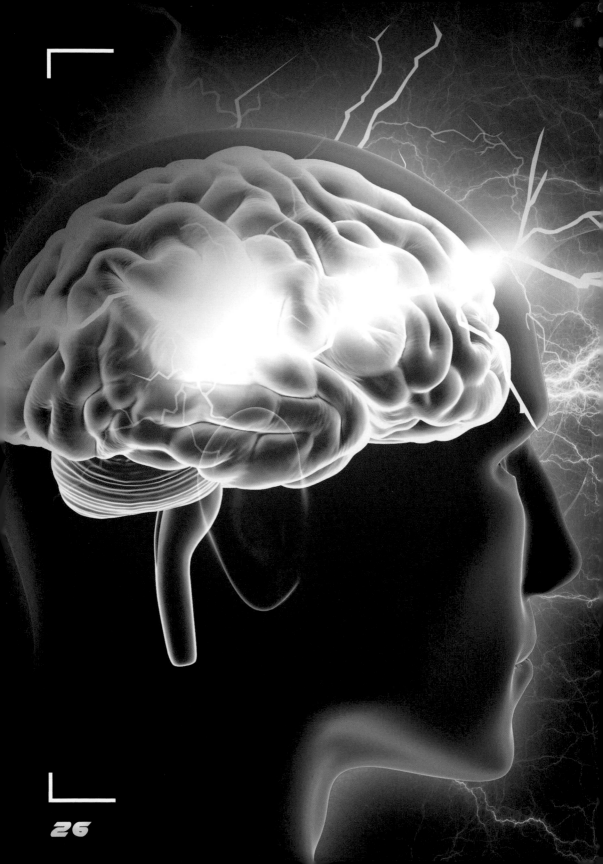

HIDDEN HINTS

The human brain is always processing
information. We often do not notice most of it.
But when we use this "hidden" information to
make guesses or predictions, we are using our
intuition. Some people might mistake strong
intuition for ESP.

Some people fake ESP for fame or money.
But many truly believe they have powers.
They feel their experiences are too strange to
be explained by chance. Skeptics disagree.
They argue that with more than 7 billion people
on the planet, any unlikely thing can happen.

For example, the more **predictions** a psychic
makes, the better the odds that one will come
true. When that happens, it is easy to forget that
the rest did not. People often focus on events that
match their beliefs.

ASK AGAIN LATER

There is still much to discover about ESP. Some studies present evidence that these abilities exist. But skeptics and believers disagree on what the results mean. Researchers need more data and stronger methods to move forward.

Parapsychologists continue to seek answers. In 2014, the U.S. government began a new research program. It studies sailors and soldiers that seem to have a sixth sense for danger. Programs like these could reveal exciting new information about ESP. But for now, it remains a mystery. Do you see answers in our future?

GLOSSARY

clairvoyants—people who are able to feel things outside the five senses; clairvoyants often communicate with spirits or predict future events.

Cold War—the conflict between the United States and the former Soviet Union that lasted from 1947 to 1991

data—facts or information used to study or make sense of something

electroencephalograph—a device that detects and records the electrical activity of the brain

evidence—information that helps prove or disprove something

ganzfeld experiments—experiments used to study ESP in which the subject's sight and hearing are blocked

hit—a response that correctly matches the target in an ESP study

investigate—to try to find out the facts about something in order to learn if or how it happened

parapsychologist—a person who studies events that cannot be explained by what scientists know about nature and the world

predictions—statements about what will or might happen in the future

pupil—the area at the center of the eye where light enters

receptors—nerve endings that allow the body to process the five senses

remote viewing—the practice of using ESP to gather information on someone, or something, unseen or far away

skeptics—people who doubt something is true

Spiritualism—a religion that claims ghosts can communicate with living people

subjects—people used in experiments or studies

telepathy—a way of communicating thoughts directly from one person's mind to another person's mind without using words or signals

white noise—a constant noise that is a mixture of many different sound waves, such as the sound of static on a radio

TO LEARN MORE

AT THE LIBRARY

Borgert-Spaniol, Megan. *ESP: Does a Sixth Sense Exist?*
Minneapolis, Minn.: Abdo Pub., 2019.

Olson, Elsie. *Are You Psychic?: Facts, Trivia, and Quizzes.*
Minneapolis, Minn.: Lerner Publications, 2018.

Troupe, Thomas Kingsley. *Extreme Stories About ESP.* Mankato,
Minn.: Black Rabbit Books, 2019.

ON THE WEB

FACTSURFER

Factsurfer.com gives you
a safe, fun way to find
more information.

1. Go to www.factsurfer.com.

2. Enter "ESP" into the search box and click 🔍.

3. Select your book cover to see a list
   of related web sites.

INDEX